THINK ABOUT IT!

Let the Thinking Begin!

Thinkaboutit! Philosophy For Kids (Let the Thinking Begin!)
Second Edition published by Enable Training and Consulting Inc.
Three Hundred Bronte Street South, Milton, Ont.

The author acknowledges the generous assistance of the Ontario Arts Council in the form of a Writer's Reserve grant.

ONTARIO ARTS COUNCIL
CONSEIL DES ARTS DE L'ONTARIO

International Standard Book Number: 978-1-927425-10-7

Author: Amy Leask
Design and Illustration: Mark Hughes
Contributor: Katy Leask
Editor, Publisher: Ben Zimmer

Enable Training and Consulting
300 Bronte St. S., Unit 1
Milton, Ont., Canada L9T 1Y8
905.864.1858
1.877.872.4619
www.enabletc.com
www.kidsthinkaboutit.com

For Ruby, and all other amazing little thinkers.

Enable
Training and Consulting, Inc.

Say Hello to Philosophy!

Hi! I'm Sophia, and I think I have the coolest name in the world. Sophia means wisdom, and wisdom is what people have when they think great ideas. My name suits me just fine, because thinking great ideas just happens to be one of my favorite things to do. I'm not just Sophia, but "Sophia the Wise"!

We all think. It's as normal as breathing or eating. We all have crazy little ideas zooming around in our heads like fireflies. We think while we brush our teeth. We think while we're on the bus. We even think in our sleep. Sometimes all we do is sit around and think. Whether you're a pirate, a painter, a nurse, a nectarine farmer, a chef, or a shepherd, chances are that you have at least a million thoughts floating around in your brain every day. The space between your ears can be a very busy place!

There are some people who think about very strange things. They wonder about very big ideas. I don't mean very big like a swimming pool, either. I mean very big ideas that people have wondered about since people became people.

Some people ask crazy questions, questions that don't usually have easy answers, such as:

There's a name for people who ask these big questions. They're called *philosophers* (fill-oss-uff-ers). The kind of thinking they do is called *philosophy* (fill-oss-uff-eee). As you may have noticed, my name is part of that word. A philosopher is a lover of wisdom, and really, anybody can be one. Anybody can think big ideas, and ask big questions. You've probably been doing it since your parents called you "Short Stuff". You probably used to ask them things like "Why?" over and over, until they got really irritated. You probably used to ask why the sky is blue, why elephants have big feet, and why grown-ups have strange hair coming out of their ears. Well, it's time to think big ideas and ask big questions again. This time around, you'll be taller. Turn on your brain, shake the cobwebs out of your head, and get ready to think!

ThinkAboutIt!

IN THIS ISSUE!

Hannah Arendt

Full Name: Hannah Arendt
Born: 1906 AD
Died: 1975 AD
Hometown: Hanover, Germany
Fave Subjects: Freedom, Politics
Career Highlights: wrote more than 20 books, was the first female student and first female professor at her university, worked for an organization that helped children of war

Look at this winning lineup! We have champion thinkers from Greece, England, Austria, Denmark and Germany!

Martin Buber

Full Name: Martin Buber
Born: 1878 AD
Died: 1965 AD
Hometown: Vienna, Austria
Fave Subjects: Human Relationships, Power, Religion, How Minds Work , Art
Career Highlights: wrote more than 30 books, taught people from different cultures to live together peacefully

Socrates

Full Name: Socrates
Born: 469 BC
Died: 399 BC
Hometown: Athens, Greece
Fave Subjects: Almost Everything!
Career Highlights: taught thousands of young people to think without ever writing anything down, was a teacher to Plato (another famous philosopher)

Bertrand Russell

Full Name: Bertrand Arthur William Russell
Born: 1872 AD
Died: 1970 AD
Hometown: London, England
Fave Subjects: Math, Logic, Science, Right and Wrong, Religion, Language
Career Highlights: wrote more than 60 works, created new ways to do math, stood up for peace in times of war, won a Nobel Prize for his writing

Soren Kierkegaard

Full Name: Soren Aabye Kierkegaard
Born: 1813 AD
Died: 1855 AD
Hometown: Copenhagen, Denmark
Fave Subjects: Art, Right and Wrong, Freedom, Power, Religion
Career Highlights: wrote more than 20 books, started a new type of philosophy, but preferred to think of himself as a writer, rather than a philosopher

Sophia the Wise's Rules for Doing Philosophy
(and lots of other stuff too)

1

There is no such thing as a stupid question! If you want to know something, you should ask!

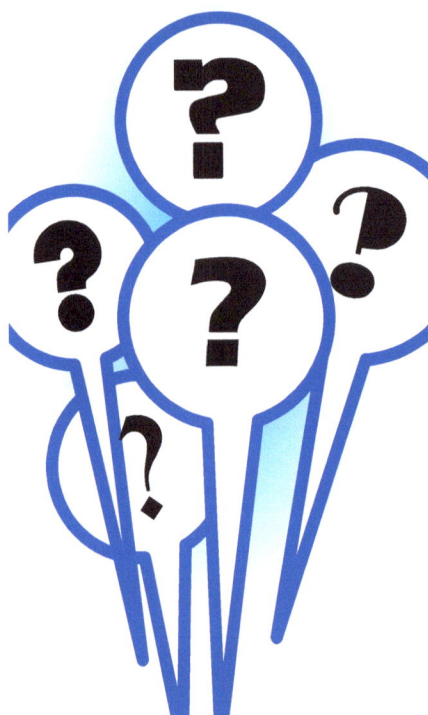

2

Share with other philosophers! Two heads are better than one. Three, four, or five heads are even better.

3

Collect as many different ideas as you can! Never throw an idea away without thinking carefully about it first.

4

Stay on track! Don't let your brain think about too many other things while you're trying to figure out the answer. Tell your brain to pay attention!

ThinkAboutIt!

5

Explain yourself! Just like you, philosophers hate it when people say "just because," or "because I said so". Tell people why you think the things you do.

6

Let other people speak! It's rude to cut people off or ignore them. You wouldn't want them to do that to you.

7

Keep your eyes peeled! Philosophy is everywhere, in books, comics, newspapers, and maybe even on the back of your cereal box.

8

Don't get angry! Some ideas in philosophy get people really excited. Keep your cool and keep on talking.

9

Write things down! If you come up with a brilliant question, or an even more brilliant answer, you'll want to remember it later.

10

Go back and visit old questions again! Sometimes you'll find a whole bunch of new answers the next time around.

ThinkAboutIt!

The Big Questions in Philosophy:

There are as many questions in philosophy as there are people to ask them, but most philosophers share a few important curiosities. You've probably wondered about things like this too.

What is real?
- Am I made of a mind and a body, or am I just a body, or just a mind?
- Do I get to choose what I do, or does something force me to act this way?
- What is it that makes each person so special and different from everyone else?

Philosophers call this *Metaphysics* (met-a-fizz-icks).

How do we know what we know?
- Can I trust my five senses to tell me the truth, or do they sometimes fool me?
- Is what's true for me true for everyone?
- Is there anything I've always known, or did I have to learn everything?

Philosophers call this *Epistemology* (ee-pist-em-all-ogee).

How do we know the difference between right and wrong?
- Should rules for "being good" be the same for everyone, or can they be different for each person?

POWER LOOKS GOOD ON ME!

- Is it ever okay to be selfish?
- Is it possible to be too good?

Philosophers call this *Ethics* (eth-icks).

How do we decide who is in charge?
- What does it mean for someone to have power?
- Should we have one person in charge, or many people in charge?
- If we want to make changes to the way people do things, what's the best way to decide how?

Philosophers call this *Politics* (poll-it-icks).

What does it mean for something to be beautiful?
- Do beauty and ugliness mean the same thing for everyone?
- What is art, anyway?
- How do people come up with new and interesting things?

Philosophers call this *Aesthetics* (a-stct-icks).

How do we make a good argument?
- Why can't we say "just because"?
- What kinds of things can we tell people to help them understand our thoughts and opinions?
- How can we make room for many different ideas?

Philosophers call this *Logic* (law-jic).

ThinkAboutIt!

What Can Philosophy Do For Me?

Okay, so far, we've seen that philosophy is interesting, but did you know that it's also very useful? There are loads of ways that philosophy can make life easier for us. Join me, Sophia the Wise, as I say hello to a few famous and important philosophers, and hear what they have to say.

According to Socrates (saw-crat-eez):
Philosophy makes us curious!

My name is Socrates, and I lived in ancient Greece about two thousand, five hundred years ago. Although some people say I'm the most famous philosopher in the western world, I never wrote any of my ideas down (luckily, one of my students did, later on). Instead, I spent my days hanging out in my toga, holding classes with young people, discussing all kinds of ideas, and trying to figure out the meaning of life. I always said "The unexamined life is not worth living." If I hadn't done philosophy, I don't know what else I would have done! I never really figured out the answers to the big questions I asked, and that was just fine with me. I believed that the smartest person was the one who could say "I don't know." Not knowing means that we will keep looking for new and exciting ideas. Philosophy is very useful because it makes us curious, and being curious helps us to have better lives.

ThinkAboutIt!

According to Mr. Buber (boo-burr): Philosophy helps us live together!

I am Martin Buber, and my time as a philosopher began in Austria, more than a hundred years ago. One of the biggest ideas I ever thought about was how people aren't ever alone in the world, and how important this is. I don't get to be good old Martin all by myself. I do it by being someone's friend, someone's family member, or the guy someone sees eating soup at a restaurant. We share our world and our lives with many other people, as well as with animals, plants and other things. We learn about ourselves by getting to know everything and everyone we meet. We can learn about ourselves by sitting near a beautiful tree, by petting a cute dog, or by talking to someone at recess. Just thinking about someone or something else, even if they're not actually there, can still teach us valuable lessons about ourselves, and about everything else. For me, philosophy is useful because it teaches us about how important relationships are.

ThinkAboutIt!

According to Mr. Kierkegaard (keer-kuh-gard): Philosophy builds our courage!

They call me Soren Kierkegaard, and I grew up in Denmark, almost two hundred years ago. Like anyone else, I was sometimes scared, worried, or not quite sure about things. However, I learned that sometimes, if something is really important and we really care about it, we shouldn't let things like fear, worry, or doubt stop us from trying. I called this "the leap of faith", meaning that sometimes we just have to "jump" into something. Hey, if we were always stopping ourselves because we weren't sure, we'd never fall in love, try a new flavor of potato chip, or sing anywhere outside of the shower. This doesn't mean we should do foolish things like shave off half of our hair, or juggle flaming kitchen knives, but it does mean that life is a little better if we aren't afraid to sometimes seek out new adventures. My friends, I am here to tell you that philosophy can teach us to be brave!

ThinkAboutIt!

According to Ms. Arendt (ah-rent):
Philosophy helps us change the world!

Hannah Arendt here, and boy, oh boy, did I learn a lot of important things from philosophy! I was born in Germany over a hundred years ago, and like a lot of philosophers, I was fascinated with the idea of having power. I spent a lot of time watching the way people boss other people around, and I decided it wasn't fair. I thought "How can people do such terrible things to others?" and I really wanted to know how to fix this. Most people do mean things without thinking about how it might affect others. Eureka! People need to learn to not listen to bullies, and to imagine what might happen if they do something to someone else. If we can teach people to really think about how their actions can hurt others, then we can start to make things better for everyone. The most useful thing I learned from philosophy was how to change the world!

ThinkAboutIt!

According to Mr. Russell (russ-ull):
Philosophy makes you a better thinker!

Bertrand Russell is my name, and I was born in England almost one hundred fifty years ago. I had a reputation for being a no-nonsense kind of philosopher, the kind that likes to think clearly and logically. In my opinion, people don't think enough. When they do think, they often believe things because it makes them happy, or because someone else says it's true. I understand why this happens. Thinking well can be quite difficult. Sometimes it means admitting that we're wrong, and no one likes to be wrong. It also means that we spend a lot of time not being sure about anything, and having to keep looking for more and more information, but it's all good. Good thinking isn't about being a know-it-all who has everything figured out. It's about being a want-to-know-it-all who never stops looking for better ideas. Philosophy is useful because it teaches us to think better. It sounds like a small thing, but it's very important!

ThinkAboutIt!

Philosophers Behaving WEIRDLY

Even with their amazing ideas, philosophers are still human beings, and human beings do some crazy, strange, and fascinating things. For example:

Empress Wu (woo) had some of her family members thrown in jail (or worse) so she could become leader of China.

Sometimes when Baruch Spinoza (spin-oh-zah) got bored, he'd stick flies on spider webs and watch them squirm. Eeeeew!

Immanuel Kant (cant) was so organized that his neighbours would set their clocks by his morning walks.

Simone Weil's (vay) friends thought she was so strange that they nicknamed her "The Martian".

Jean-Paul Sartre (sar-truh) was afraid of being chased by lobsters. It must have been the pinchers!

ThinkAboutIt!

David Hume started university when he was only twelve years old! Smarty Pants!

Diogenes (di-oj-en-ees) was a grouch who hated other people so much that he spent years living in a barrel on the street. I wonder where he put the refrigerator?

William James was tone deaf. It's a good thing he didn't grow up to be a rock star!

Renee Descartes (day-cart) was the annoying kid in class who couldn't stop asking questions, and he drove his teachers crazy with his, "Oooh, oooh! Pick me! Pick me!"

In addition to being a philosopher, Ayn Rand wrote and acted in Hollywood movies. Lights! Camera! Think!

ThinkAboutIt!

THINKING IS AN EXTREME SPORT!

Other Cool Questions in Philosophy:

Philosophy is like a snowball, rolling downhill. It just gets bigger and bigger as it moves along. Just in case you still haven't had enough big ideas for one day (or if you have an extra-large brain), here are a few more questions that philosophers love to ask.

1. Why does it sometimes seem like time goes slowly (like when you're at the dentist), and other times (like when you're playing with the cat), it seems to go faster? Shouldn't time always be the same? Is it possible to travel forward or backward in time?

2. What's the difference between humans and animals? Are we really so different from creatures that crawl, fly, or swim? Is it right or wrong to eat meat, knowing that it comes from animals? Why do we keep some animals as pets, and other animals as food?

3. Can robots be just like humans? Can we make robots that can feel, think, and act just like people do, or will they always be a little bit different? How do you know that people you meet aren't robots?

ThinkAboutIt!

WHAT FOOLS THESE HUMANS BE!

4. Why do we think boys and girls are so different? Are there really things that boys can do that girls can't, or vice versa? Is it all in our imagination?

5. If you do something wrong, and nobody finds out about it, is it still wrong? Does keeping things a secret make them all right? Is it always best to be honest with people?

6. If you could make a copy of yourself, would you want to? Would the copy of you be the same as the original you? How could you tell the difference?

7. Is there anything that has always been around? Is there anything that doesn't have a beginning, or anything that will never end?

8. What does it mean to love something or someone? What's the difference between liking and loving?

9. What does it mean for something to be "normal"? Does it mean that it's something that we're used to, or does it mean something else?

ThinkAboutIt!

10. What does it mean to be happy? Is it the same thing as being famous, smart, rich or lucky? What do we need in order to have a good life?

11. If an alien came down from outer space and didn't speak your language, could you explain to him or her what it means to be a human being? What kinds of ideas do you think you could share with someone from a whole other part of the universe?

12. Do science and technology teach us everything we need to know about the world, or should we study other things too?

13. If you could design your own school, one that would help students to learn more, what would it be like?

And the list goes on, and on, and on…

ThinkAboutIt!

*Translation:
So is this!

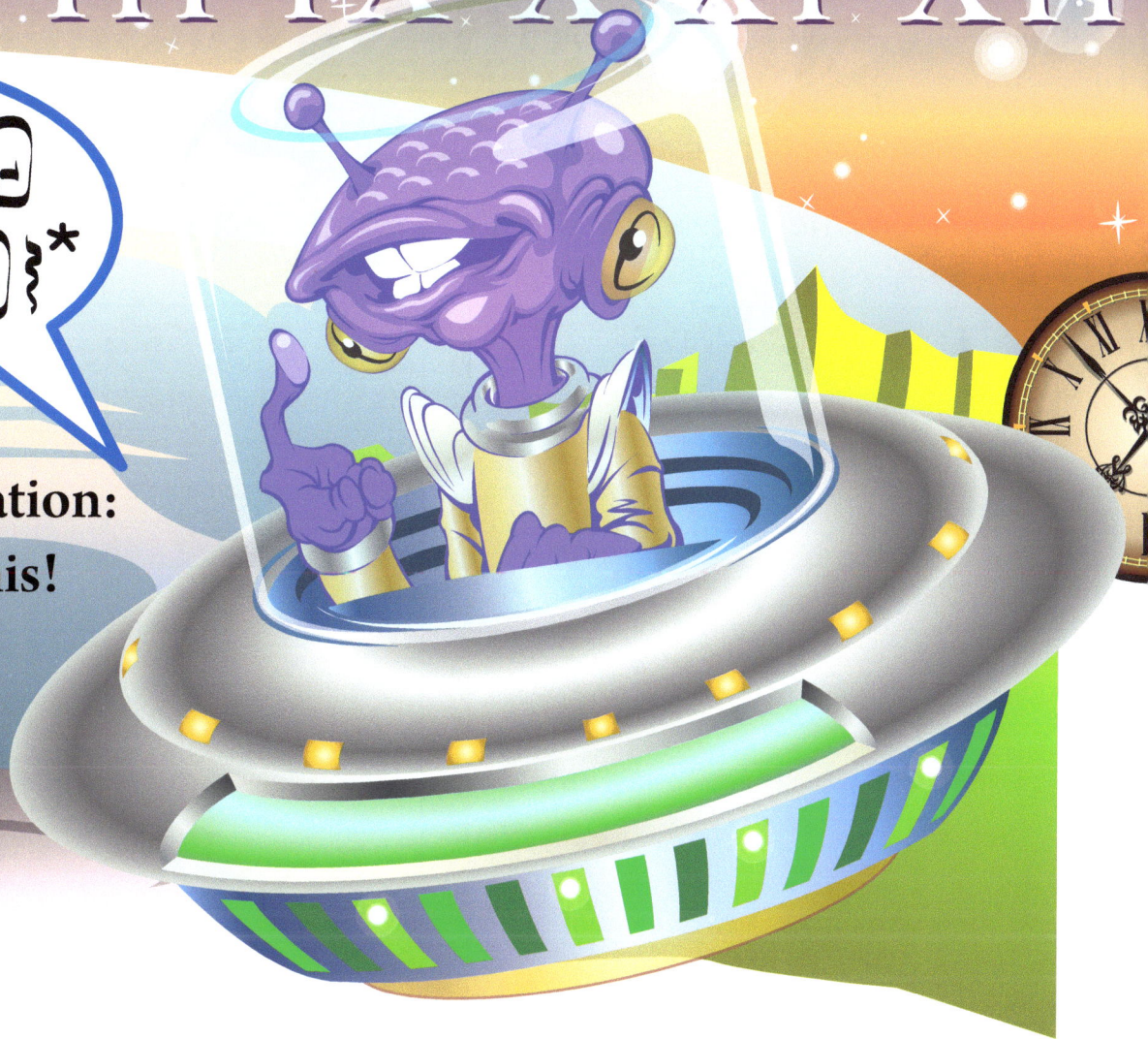

So, What Now?

Whew! That was a lot of big ideas, and a lot of heavy thinking, even for Sophia The Wise. Does your head hurt? Do you have big ideas of your own? The really great thing about philosophy is that for every big question, there are a million possible answers. Even better, we can always invent our own new questions. Philosophers have been doing this stuff for thousands of years, and no one's really figured it all out yet. The important thing is to keep thinking, and talking, and thinking and talking some more. Do some deep thinking while you're combing your hair! Throw around some big ideas while you're playing fetch with the dog! Ask yourself enormous questions when you're at school, when you're on your bike, or when you're at the movies! Share philosophy with your friends, your family, and new people you meet! Who knows, maybe someday you will grow up to be a great thinker too!

ThinkAboutIt!

The BIGGEST Question

The biggest question I've ever wanted answered is:

The answer could be...	Or the answer could be...
Maybe the answer is...	It's possible that the answer is...

ThinkAboutIt!

Philosopher's Journal

Date: _____

Choose one big question from page 18 - 20 and think about it a little bit each day for one week

The big question I chose is...

Write or draw your big thoughts in the bubbles below.

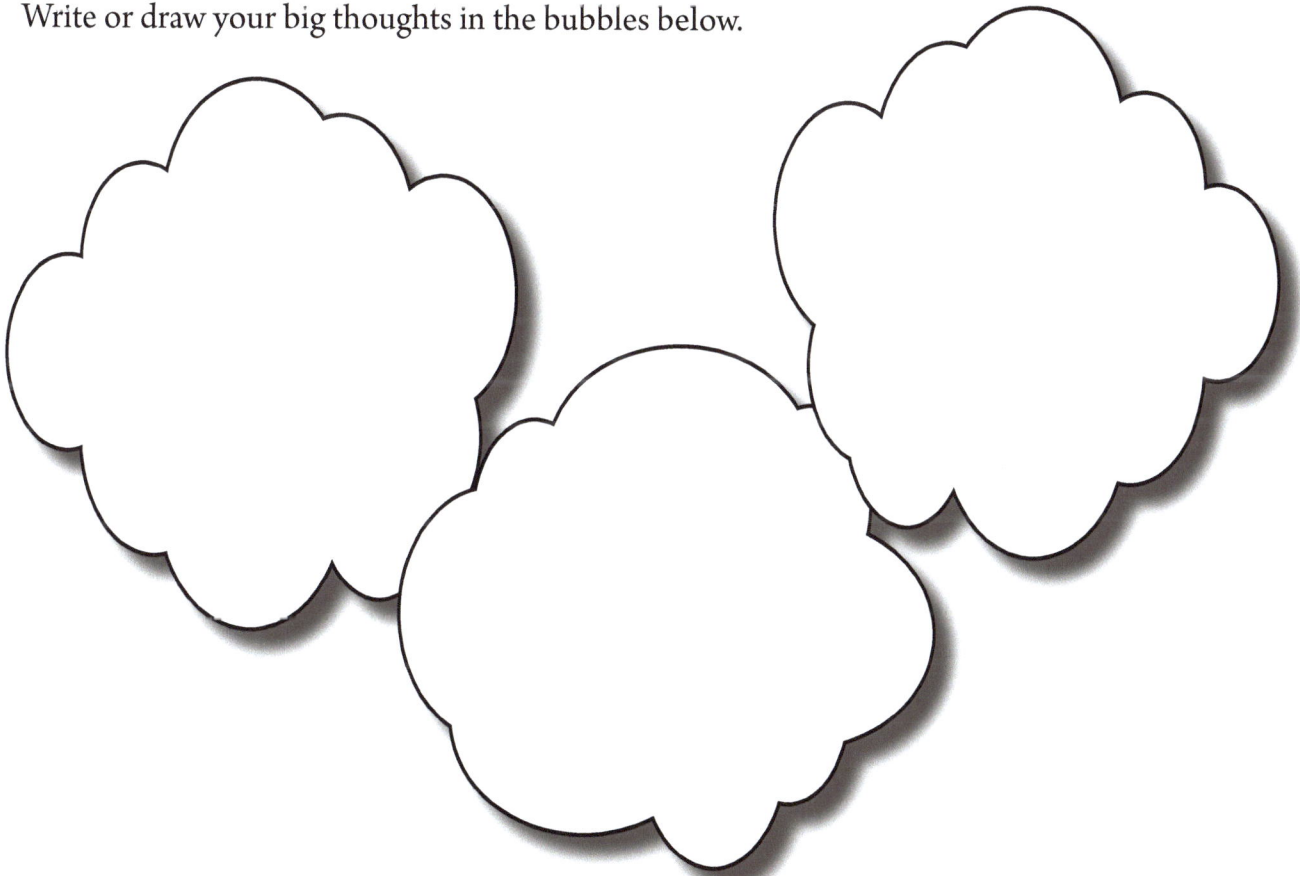

Did this big question make you think of any other big questions? What were they?

Even a great philosopher can always learn more (just ask Socrates)! Now that you know a little bit about philosophy, what else would you like to find out? Are there other big questions you'd like answered? Do you want to find out more about a particular thinker, or what it was like to do philosophy in a different time or place? Write down or draw your thoughts!

Journal Of Thoughts

Name: _____   Date: _____

ThinkAboutIt!

Kierkegaard

Arendt

Russell

Buber

Socrates

Color It In!

World Locations of
Famous
Philosophers

A Timeline of Great Philosophical Minds

(...and a brief history of the world)

Socrates 	469-399BC	• Celtic settlers kick off the Iron Age in the British Isles. • In Athens, Greece, the Parthenon is completed, including a thirty-eight-foot gold statue of the goddess Athena. Bling! Bling! • Nehemiah and Ezra build the Wall of Jerusalem (and people's courage).
Kierkegaard 	1813-1855 AD	• Scottish inventor Kirkpatrick Macmillan introduces the bicycle. The wheelie is invented much later. • University degrees are granted to American women. Girl power! • Japan begins to welcome outside visitors. On your left, Mount Fuji...
Russell 	1872-1970 AD	• China abolishes slavery. Sweet freedom! • The first refrigerator is sold in Sweden, and lovers of leftovers rejoice! • Television is invented by American engineer Philo Farnsworth, and the couch potato is born.
Buber 	1878-1965 AD	• The Kingdom of Saudi Arabia is founded, with more than a million square miles of sun and sand. • World War 2 begins (and ends, thank goodness). • Ghana becomes the first African state to win independence. Great stuff for the Gold Coast!
Arendt 	1906-1975 AD	• Gandhi helps India win its independence, and still finds time to make his own clothes. • Jonas Salk creates the polio vaccine. Take that, nasty disease! • Neil Armstrong is the first human to walk (more like bounce) on the moon.

www.ingramcontent.com/pod-product-compliance
Lightning Source LLC
Chambersburg PA
CBHW042112040426
42448CB00002B/232